$\mathcal{D}$EFEAT

WAS NEVER

AN

OPTION

EVANGELIST JOANNA BIRCHETT

ISBN 978-0-9831637-3-2

Library of Congress Control Number: 2012937549

First Edition Printing

**Printed In the United States of America
April 2012**

For more information about Evangelist Joanna Birchett
please visit: www.gospel4uministry.com

For bookings and speaking engagements email
gospel4uministry@gmail.com

CONTENTS

FOREWORD

To God be the glory for all the He's doing in the life of my wife, Evangelist Joanna Birchett. It is a great delight and honor to write anything that will precede the anointed and uplifting pages that will follow in this book, Defeat Was Never an Option.

I truly believe that the topic of this body of work is so appropriate and on time not only for the unbeliever but for those of us that normally consider ourselves to be included in "Christendom". We as men and women of God are so easily defeated in this day and time and it's time for someone to sound the alarm that *No, in all these things we are more than conquerors through him who loved us. Romans 8:37 (NIV).*

Not only is defeat not an option for us we have to understand that it was never intended to be an option. God tells us in His Word that we are more than conquerors and even asks us the question *if God is for us, who can be against us? Romans 8:31 (NIV).* Being as though the result of both of these scriptures leads us to understand the nature of the power that lies within us through God is Victors because we're victorious. We have to defeat every opposition that comes against what God says is ours!

Saints, Evangelist Joanna Birchett, breaks down the Word of God so eloquently and beautifully in this book that by the end you will have a holy boldness that will cause the Kingdom of Darkness to tremble because you will be able to go on the battlefield of your life and look at Goliath and say today I will kill you, cut your head off, and go back to fulfilling the purpose of my life.

I unashamedly, recommend that this book of devotions, inspiring thoughts, and direct words from the Lord be read and reread on a daily basis because it comes from a place so deep inside Joanna that it is easily one of the most powerful books to be released in this generation. As her husband I personally know that a lot of these chapters were written in tears as she toiled with the Lord as to whether she should be as transparent as she is about her own life in the pages of this book. Joanna has an awesome prayer life and worships God in such a way that I believe it makes angels jealous. This is the kind of person that is behind the words of this book.

Be blessed as you maneuver through the awesome chapters ahead and again, to God be all the Glory for the things that He's about to do in your life. God bless you and remember Defeat Was Never an Option!

Rev. Larry E. Birchett, Jr.
President/Founder
Treasures of the Heart International Ministries

ACKNOWLEDGEMENT

I first want to give all Glory to the Lord who made this possible.

A very special thank you to my wonderful and anointed Husband, Larry Birchett, Jr. This man has fully supported in and through every venture that I have taken. I can truly say that he is my best friend and mentor. Larry I love you and I know you have my back.

Thank you to my children who had to bear with me not paying attention sometimes because I was so busy trying to get this project accomplished, I love you guys.

Thank you to my Pastors Earl and Maria Palmer who always has the right words to encourage me.

There are a few people that I would love to acknowledge and I want to publicly thank, Rebecca Rush, who always pours into my spirit and encouraged me to pursue my dreams.

To Kim Allen who has been there for me more ways than one.

Cala Allison, I don't have words to express how you have impacted my life and I thank God that you are my friend.

To Iris Rodriquez, a woman who the Lord placed in my life for such a time as this.

To Jennifer Marlowe, you are a true blessing in my life and a great friend. I can call you any time of the night and you are there.

I would like to thank my mother in law, Arlene Birchett for allowing the Lord to touch her heart and bring me in to praise Dance at any given time, because of this I realize that I can do anything the Lord desires of me, thank you Mom B.

To everyone that has encouraged me and prayed for me over the years, I am blessed to have great support and I am forever grateful.

To Pastor Ayanna, publisher and dear friend, I want to say thank you for allowing the Lord to use you to be a blessing to me at a time when I needed it the most. We were divinely connected and I am so excited for what the Lord has in store.

DEDICATION

This book is dedicated to my Lord and Savior Jesus Christ. It is because of His love for me that I am able to release this book, and for this I am forever grateful!

He was Always There

For the LORD will not forsake His people for His great name's sake: because it hath pleased the LORD to make you His people. ~ 1 Samuel 12:22

My life has gone through many different seasons. Like a lot of people I did not grow up in the church and I did a lot of things that should have excluding me from being used by God but I give Him all the glory because He saw fit to save me from all the mess that I was in and revealed His plan for my life. So I can't help but to give Him all glory and all credit for all that He has done and all He is still doing!

My life was not always this way, and I was not always saved, but because of the grace and mercy of Jesus I am have delivered and set free!

I grew up in the beautiful Island of Jamaica and at the age of eighteen I migrated to the United States. I ended up in the windy city, Chicago, but for some strange reason I always knew that this was not going to be my final destination.

I took a detour in my life because I wanted to fit in with the Jones'. Life will take you where your heart leads and because I wanted to be popular I found myself barking up the wrong tree which led to me getting pregnant at an early age. As you might already know doing things the way we want comes with a high price.

I left Chicago and ended up in Philadelphia, and this is where it all began. I made wrong choices for my life; Clubs, selling drugs, driving fancy cars were all in my vocabulary and nobody could tell me different. *You know you are wrong when you don't want your parents or kids to know where your source of survival comes from.*

Let me tell you all, I should have been dead a long time ago BUT GOD! Yes even when I strayed away in the wrong direction He was always my Shepherd, watching over me. I was making crazy money and it was so easy for me. Don't you know that sin is enticing and so easy to get in but so hard to get out? It makes you believe that the grass is greener on the other side and once you step your foot on that side you find out you have been deceived.

Let me share this with you, the Bible says that if you make your bed in hell even there will the Lord be with you. I remember one time when I was about twenty years old living with my son's dad, I was home alone with my son and step kids and we heard a loud banging on the door, it was the police!

They were there to seize everything and everyone that was illegal. At this point of my life I actually had no knowledge of what was going on, *but what a friend we have in Jesus* because it seems as though an angel was watching over me! They left us at the house after they tore everything apart and even gave me money to order pizza for the kids and told us they were not going to harm us they were not looking for us.

Isn't it amazing how God always has His hands on you, even when you are not in His will? I lost my home, my family was torn apart but God had a purpose and a plan throughout it all. I am so glad that He never gave up on me, so that is why I cannot allow the enemy to place "Defeat" in my life. Sometimes in life we allow a temporary situation to be permanent when that is not the will of God for our life.

There is nothing that you or anyone can tell me about the streets because I lived it, and I have lived to make Thousands of Dollars and end up with zero, the Bible says *What does it profit a man to gain the whole world and lose his soul?* (Mark 8:36)

I can tell you, NOTHING... I was on my way to hell and thought that the life I was living was IT. But thanks be to God He did not allow me to die in New York when I got robbed of $80,000.00 and had a trash bag placed over my head to kill me! *Even in my mess God was there all the time.* Yes He was, so when I look back over my life I say to myself "Lord, Defeat will Never be an option for me"

I cannot give up when He has so much for me to do. So many lives are being wasted and yet we find time to hate on each other and lie on each other. I urge you today to get it together don't worry about getting rich quick or trying to trick someone out of their birthright but know that wherever you are the Lord will meet you if you only give your life to Him and surrender all.

He is omnipotent and omnipresent; He is always watching over you, He is EL-ROI: The God that sees.

Alone but Never Lonely

And Jesus withdrew Himself into the wilderness, and prayed. ~ Luke 5:16

This is geared to everyone who is single, divorced or widowed, although I am now married I do have experience in being alone. I served as the Single's president for three years in my local church and lived as a single mother for over 19 years, so trust me I know the things that you go through; **Hardship, Temptation, Struggles.**

In the book of 1Cor. 7:7 Paul clearly states that Singleness is a gift from the Lord and not everyone handles that gift, well! It is clear that some people are single for a season, single by choice, single from divorce, or even from being widowed.

As a single woman, it can get hard, pressuring, frustrating and even sometimes discouraging. But the Bible says in Isaiah 26:3 *"You will keep him in perfect peace, whose mind is stayed on you, because he trusts in you."* I remember when I used to look to men for my source, oh yes! I had to learn the hard way, but one thing I try to always understand was that even when I had a man of my own, I still felt lonely and alone. God had to show me that a man cannot fill the voids; he cannot complete me, because he is not God! We must first ask the Lord to give us a new mindset.

Let me tell you about the mind friends, the mind is a terrible thing to waste; it will let you perceive what's not as though it is, so you have to meditate on the WORD. You must Trust in God, even when you don't understand what He's doing, JUST TRUST HIM, He has allowed you to be single for a reason, nothing takes Him by surprise! He is always there for you and it does not matter the mess you are in He can clean you up, turn you around. He can turn a dancehall queen into an Evangelist, a prostitute into a prophetess, a pimp into a Pastor, oh Yes He can!

Don't let the fact that you got pregnant at sixteen stop you. God will restore you. You should be happy about that because the fact that you are reading my book, lets you know that He kept me even when I had no desire to be kept! I am alive today all because of His GRACE AND MERCY and if He did if for me He surely can and will do it for you. If you don't believe let me share this with you.

About 12 years ago I was dating someone who had a girlfriend, long story short, I got jumped by her and her friends with machete and I was placed on a video that slandered my character. I never knew that I would have come out of that situation alive. I was not saved, sanctified or filled with the Holy Spirit, but I knew there was a God. It was during those times that I experienced being alone and feeling lonely, during those times I went into a cave of low self-esteem, bitterness, unforgiveness and you can keep naming them, so I know what it feels like to be out there feeling like there is no hope. There is a saying; *you don't know what people go through until you been through it.*

According to Dictionary definition "Loneliness is a feeling of separation, isolation, or distance in human relations. Loneliness implies emotional pain, an empty feeling, and a yearning to feel understood and accepted by someone."

Our greatest test in life is how we will obey the will of God to put aside our own selves and truly lose ourself in Him. I remember when I was single and my flesh would literally speak to me, I would feel like I always had to have companion. I messed up even while I was in the Church, I would do my thing and come into the house of God in an act of Worship. God was not pleased with my actions and He allowed me to go through a season of solitude, a time when I had no one around and it was then that He was able to get my attention. This was my wilderness experience. Please don't believe for a moment that I don't know what you go through, my sister, my brother, you cannot allow a lonely season to cause you to miss the move of God or to miss your breakthrough because seasons do change! I can declare to the world that even in these times I never gave up and you can overcome too.

Here are four pointers I would like to leave with you:

1. **You must be sold out for the Lord** – Seek ye first the Kingdom of Heaven and its righteousness Matthew 6:33

2. **You must be content** – 1 Timothy 6:6 (Godliness with contentment is great gain)

3. **Be confident about who you are** – Lack of self-confidence leads to loneliness, you are a child of the most high God and you are blessed and highly favored. You might be single now but you don't know what tomorrow holds, the bible says in Jeremiah 29:11...

For I know the plans I have for you, declares the Lord, plans to prosper you and not to harm you, plans to give you hope and a future.

4. **Must build good character** – Proverbs 31 He wants to build good character in us, so that even if you are Alone you know that He is there with you always and there will not be any room for loneliness.

Whatever season you are in right now, just know that God is still in control.

Hebrews 13:5 says *I will never leave you nor forsake you.*

Singleness is to be embraced, celebrated, and used as a time to grow closer to the Lord. Get a made up mind and know that you might not have a natural companion but God is always with you and even us married folks still need God!

I know you might be single reading this and you might be saying well, Joanna you are married and you don't know how hard it is, Well I wasn't always married so I know exactly what it feels like! But I also learned how to embrace and learn from my season of being single. Don't you know that *now* is the time to discover wholeness in your single life while God is preparing you to be a wife or husband!!!

~I will not leave you comfortless: I will come to you.~
John 14:18

My Blessings

For I know the thoughts that I think toward you,
saith the LORD, thoughts of peace, and not of evil, to
give you an expected end~ Jeremiah 29:11

There are so many things that the Lord has delivered me from, things that I know I was not supposed to be a part of, but I want to give glory to God that even in those times when I was not serving Him the way I should He kept me for such a time as this.

Sometimes I feel like Esther, because if I perish I perish! But whatever the Lord says that shall I do, even now being saved there are people that hate me for no cause but if you live long enough you will learn that people don't like to see you up, they would prefer to see you at your lowest, looking to them for help.

I used to always wonder why people lied on me or disliked me for no apparent reason. I asked the Lord those questions and after so many years of wondering the Lord used Rebecca, a dear friend of mine, to tell me that I was being attacked because there is greatness locked up on the inside, she said to me, "Joe, I don't believe that all the hell that you are going through is in vain, God has a purpose and a plan."

I say this to say that your blessing comes in many ways, but you cannot get weary in well doing, you have to fight the enemy with everything in you because defeat is **not** in your vocabulary.

I must say that even while I was saved I almost got married to the wrong person because of a certain need, but when you have a relationship with GOD He will keep you if you want to be kept.

Yes, I really mean that! I remember one night the Lord woke me up a day before I almost made the worst mistake of my life, I was about to marry the wrong man, *what a chaos that would have been!*

The Lord woke me up at 3 am and I heard Him tell me NO! At first, I did not understand so I kept trying to go back to sleep but all I heard was NO! I realized the Lord was trying to tell me something and when you are a child of God you recognize His voice.

I immediately got up and called a friend of mine and told her that the wedding was off I cannot do it. She was thinking I was crazy but I explained everything to her and she prayed with me and the next day I broke it off.

A few months later a friend of mine told me "Joanna, until you become content with your life right now and wait on the Lord you will keep missing your blessings." I want to let you know that after she said that my whole mindset changed, I became more effective in my ministry (Singles Ministry) and it was when I took my mind off the things of my flesh started toiling in the field like Ruth, not paying any attention to anything but God that He opened the flood gates of Heaven and sent me my BOAZ, Larry Birchett, Jr.

Don't believe for one moment that it was easy, the waiting process is your test of faith and If you can hold on and trust in the Lord, believe me, it will all work together for your good.

If I should leave anything with you today just know that your blessing comes from God, your promotion comes from God, your breakthrough comes from God, and man cannot stop what God has ordained from the foundation of the Earth, all you have to do is TOTAL SURRENDER!

Surrender your will today because everything that happens in your life is what God says it is.

Character Counts

A GOOD name is rather to be chosen than great riches, and loving favour rather than silver and gold. Proverb 22:1

Good Character! Umm... I asked the Lord how can a wretch like me have good character, after all that I have been through, after all the mess I was in. Talking about my past, I know without a doubt that it is the Lord that has directed me to put pen to paper because everything comes naturally.

I can remember a time in my life when I would be in the clubs, dancing and giving glory to the devil. I thought that this was the life driving from Philadelphia to New York every Monday night, getting dressed in my car with a group of ladies tagging along.

We did this *every* Monday night and it felt like nothing because our flesh was being satisfied, but that's all it was giving in to the flesh.

Once I had given my life to Christ and thought about all I done, I started feeling like my past would affect my future and how people would look at me. Then the Lord spoke to me and said "Joanna, There is now **no** condemnation to them that are in Christ Jesus." He assured me that I should never have any fear of giving my testimony because He allowed me to have a hurtful past so that my future would be successful. This was the beginning of building up good character in Christ.

Let's talk a little about good character, In the Book of Proverbs 31 vs. 10-31 the Lord gives us a great example of a woman with good character, a woman of wisdom, I believe that it's the Lord's desire for His women to be women of greatness. Ladies, we must believe and know that we are mighty women of God who are destined for greatness, we are women of purpose and virtue. Meaning, we must be women of excellence and of good character.

After carefully meditating on these scriptures I realized that the writer never spoke once about how this woman looked, but instead he spoke very highly of her character. Being children of God we must have Good character.

Quit thinking about what's wrong with you and

start thinking about what's right with you!

Quit thinking about how big your problem is and start dwelling on the fact of how big your God is!

God wants to use you NOW my friends and He is building character in you. Remember anything that you build takes a process and it is during the process that we are tempted to get impatient at times but if we endure and go through with the right attitude in the end the results will be Amazing!

Don't let the enemy steal your joy or delay your blessings. Get in line and in tune with the Spirit of God,

Like Ruth, get attached with a Naomi, accountability is very important!

Be bold like Esther! She decided that if she perished she would perish but she was going to see the king!

Keep your body like Mary! She recognized her body was the temple of the Holy Spirit.

Change your perception of yourself and remember good things come to those who wait because they that wait on the Lord, He shall renew their strength.

I might not always be a great judge of character but that's why I rely on the Holy Spirit who gives me the Spirit of Discernment to know the difference, you too have access to all the benefits that come with being a man or woman of God.

Allow the Lord to refine your character so even those who have the Holy Spirit and discernment will see Him through you.

Renewed Mindset

And be not conformed to this world: but be ye transformed by the renewing of your mind, that ye may prove what is that good, and acceptable, and perfect, will of God~ Romans 12:2

Every year as we embark into a New Year it is a custom for some people to make resolutions. They look at the New Year as a time of New Beginnings and will often have a catch phase or slogan to describe that year. After being in Church for so long I realize that although we may different slogans for each New Year, those slogans or resolutions are not going to stop trials or opposition from arising.

As a matter of fact it seems like the more excited we are about going into the New Year and beginning a fresh the more the attacks come during that year! I now understand that it is not about our resolutions or about the New Year but the enemy is trying to attack us so we do not have a *new mindset*. The enemy launches these attacks so that we can think, act, and respond how we use to. It took me really getting the scripture that says *Greater is He that's in me than he that is in the World* for my mindset to begin to get renewed.

A renewed mindset believes: WE CAN OVERCOME ANYTHING, THERE IS NOTHING THAT TAKES GOD BY SURPRISE THAT HE HAS NOT EQUIPPED US TO HANDLE.

I have come to the realization that I have to ask the Lord to renew my Mind because I am more than a Conqueror whether I *feel* like I am or not.

There was a time in my life when I would be easily troubled and would easily lose track of what I was supposed to doing. It took the Holy Ghost leading and guiding me into all truth for me to have a renewed mindset and to rise above my natural situations and oppositions.

To God be the glory, I have now evolved above the dream killers, above the haters and will never allow anyone or anything to cause a delay in my blessings again. I have learned that you cannot think poverty and expect wealth, you cannot think the worst and expect the best, know who you are as a child of the most high God, speak life at all times and allow room for growth.

This process was not easy! I remember about 4 years ago right after I had got married, I got a letter that I was being deported back to Jamaica due to my visa being expired, my heart sank and the devil tried to let me believe that this was it and that I was going back to where the Lord brought me out of but let me help someone out there today, *It ain't over until GOD say it's over.* There is power in the name of **JESUS!**

According to what people thought, I was not supposed to be here today but I thank the Lord for blessing me with a man of God that knows how to reach the heart of the Lord, because my faith was being tried in a BIG way and I felt like giving up.

Sometimes you will find out that when you are at your lowest valley God will step in and He is always on time! It was during my times of fasting and praying the Holy Spirit spoke to me and let me know that The Heart of the King is in the hands of the Lord, but I had to change my thinking, in order to really receive it, believe it and see it come to pass. My brother and sisters in order for you win any battle it is first won in your MIND!!

The Bible says in the book of Philippians 2:5 *Let this mind be in you, which was also in Christ Jesus,* maybe you are reading this book and have no knowledge as to what it means to renew your mind and You say, Joanna how do I get the Mind of Christ?

In order for you to have the Mind of Christ you have to surrender your life to Him and have KNOWLEDGE of who He is, you have to build a relationship with Him through spending time quality time with Him praying, reading and meditating on His word. It AFTER you have Meditated on the word and hidden it in your heart *(meaning it really becomes a part of you and you make decisions based on the Word you know)* that the Word will become alive in you and it will change your mind set which will change your life.

You cannot think poverty and expect wealth, you cannot think victory and act defeated, Nobody said the road would be easy but with God all things are POSSIBLE, Don't you know that His WORD cannot return to Him void? If He said He will do it and it will come to pass! When crisis hit and you feel as though God has abandoned you, *Don't lose hope just know you are more than a conqueror.*

Conquer means "to triumph, to overcome, to win, to succeed or to be victorious."

It was God's grace and unmerited favor that kept my mind and He is still keeping me even now! When so called friends and even family talked about me His mercy kept me. People have placed me at the bottom of the list because they thought that I was not "GOOD ENOUGH" but I love the way the Bible says, *But God chose the foolish things of the world to confound (confuse) the wise ~ 1 Corinthians 1:27*

Here are 4 pointers that might help you to know that you have the victory and I try to utilize them on a daily basis

1. The adversary is defeated and can no longer triumph in our lives. **This is our victory!**

2. No matter what you have done or how you may have failed in the past, you are more than a conqueror through Christ Jesus. Don't ever forget it. There is now no condemnation to them that are in Christ Jesus. He knew all about you and yet He still chose you..

3. You have to see yourself standing in the attacks of the enemy and **overcoming all of them**. Each and every battle is won in your mind! Cast down thoughts of defeat because they have come from the enemy and allow your mind to think thoughts of victory because you know they come from God.

4. Whatever you speak that shall you get, There is a quote that I read that stuck in my mind and it was from Kenneth Copeland, he said "**you are the prophet of your own life**" and that has stuck with me ever since.

I dare you stop right now and prophesy to yourself, despite how you feel or even how the situation might look you are **More Than A Conqueror, You are The Head and not the tail.** Speak Life Now into your situation. Don't worry about what happened yesterday, consider what God has done and is doing today!

Look that situation in the face and let it know you serve a big God, He is:

JEHOVAH-ROHI...   "The Lord my Shepherd"

JEHOVAH-SHAMMAH...   "The Lord who is present"

JEHOVAH-RAPHA...   "The Lord our Healer"

JEHOVAH-JIREH...   "The Lord will provide"

JEHOVAH-NISSI...   "The Lord our Banner"

JEHOVAH-SHALOM...   "The Lord is Peace"

EL-ELYON...   "The Most High God

EL-ROI ...   "The Strong One who sees"

EL-SHADDAI...   "God Almighty"

EL-OLAM...   "The Everlasting God"

My Brothers and Sisters He is "The Great I AM"

Omnipotent, Omnipresent God that's who He is!

When the devil tries to tell you who you are, just remember that he is an accuser of the brethren, and he will try to mess with your mind, so open your mouth and let him know that, ***Defeat is not an option in your life because you have a renewed mind!***

Having Accountability

Two are better than one; because they have a good reward for their labour. For if they fall, the one will lift up his fellow: but woe to him that is alone when he falleth; for he hath not another to help him up. ~ Ecclesiastes 4:9-10

$\mathcal{I}$Have been through so much in my life and I have learned that the greatest battles begin when you are trying to accomplish something for the Lord but despite all of that I dare you to trust in the Lord, do not be discouraged or dismayed, because this breeds defeat.

When God gives you a vision He will definitely make provision, your own will turn against you but you cannot give up, people will lie on you to the point where you cannot even prove that you are right but don't be terrified. God has great things in store for us we may just have to go through temporary challenges before we see permanent results.

When you discover your true passion you will

want to be the best you that you can and that's the Truth. Sometimes we find ourselves having a desire to do more and achieve more. There is nothing wrong with having a hunger to do more or receive more of God because I believe that God has gifted us beyond measure.

I now understand that God has called me from the time of conception, in my mother womb, the Bible says: *Before I formed thee in the belly I knew thee; and before thou camest forth out of the womb I sanctified thee, and I ordained thee a prophet unto the nations.* (Jeremiah 1:5) When I first read this very powerful scripture it felt like my whole life opened up before me.

God will reveal things to you at a time when you least expect it. My life has changed and I am now living for Jesus, walking daily with Him, but just reflecting back on some of the horrible things I went through I realize that they were needed to bring me into my destiny, all those years of struggle, sickness and pain was building character in me.

I have so much knowledge about the streets that I have no taste for the worldly things anymore and sometimes we try to help the younger generation so they don't fall into the same trap like we did, but the Lord showed me that everyone has a choice and sometimes you have to allow them to "kick their toes" or even fall down so they will learn what the Lord is teaching them, we just have to be there to pick them up.

When the Lord saved me He used a very close friend of mine, Paulette, to be there for me. She would stay with my daughter on Saturday nights while I was out partying. Paulette was a true Woman of God, she never gave up on me, she discerned then, that there was greatness on the inside of me and even with all the clubbing I did she patiently waited for the day to come when I would no longer have a taste for the world.

Paulette was there for me, her prayers were always for God to save me and use me for His Glory. It brings tears to my eyes every time I think about how the Lord used her to reach me. *Little did I know the plans of God,* I am so grateful that she never gave up on me. So you might have a sister, a friend, or even your children that has no relationship with God, my advise to you is not to give up on them, be there for them, pray for them. I am not saying that you should support their habits but accountability is key. *Try to remember where God brought you from.*

I know that some people have been in Church all their life but we all fall short at one point or the other. Falling is not the main thing, it's the getting up process, we must know that we will be tried, things will happen because we are human BUT if we shake our selves off and go to the Father He is able and just to forgive us of our sins and cleanse us of all unrighteousness, there are consequences to all our sins but the fact that we have another opportunity to ask for forgiveness is a blessing all by itself. So my brothers and sisters let us look to the hills because it's there that our help comes from.

God is not like man, He is not like us, and He will not condemn us and let us feel heavy burdened. Instead He chastises us because He loves us. He welcomes us with outstretched arms, like the story of the prodigal son in Luke 15:11-32, the father welcomed his son back home and I am here to remind you that we should have a heart that forgives, a heart that loves, and a heart that says you are my brother or my sister. God desires us to give love even loving your enemies too. Remember whatever you *give* you shall *receive* multiplied.

A Pure Heart

And he saith unto them, Are ye so without understanding also? Do ye not perceive, that whatsoever thing from without entereth into the man, it cannot defile him; Because it entereth not into the heart, but into the belly, and goeth out into the draught purging all meat. And he said, that which cometh out of the man, that defileth the man ~ Mark 7: 18-22

About 8 years ago I was at work in Center City, Philadelphia and felt numb on my left side, I was rushed to the hospital where they admitted me and diagnosed me with Cardiomyopathy which is a weakness of the heart. It was while I was laying in the hospital room that the Lord spoke to me and gave me that scripture.

We are so concerned about what to eat and what not to eat but the Lord is saying that it's not what goes in that defiles you but that which comes out. In further readings of the Scripture the Word declares that out of the mouth the heart speaks and out of the heart comes evil thoughts, theft, lying, gossiping, malice, backbiting, prophelying, pride, anger and the list goes on.

God desires us to have a heart like Him and I believe that's why He created us in His own image, He wants us to show love, be peaceful and live in unity while we speak the truth. It was then that I realized that in the natural my heart was ailing because spiritually it was a mess. I cried out to the Lord and He heard my cry and gave me a new start.

I understand that God deals with us all differently but what I am trying to say is God does not care about our connections, our appearance, or accumulated wealth, He is more concerned with our heart condition because out of the abundance of the heart the mouth shall speak.

When the Lord allows things to happen in your life it's for a reason, I realize that just like Job the Lord will instigate things in your life because He does not want us to be passive. He desires for us to be strong minded and pure in heart. I believe that there is a Judas around all of us but this does not mean that you are to treat them any different, because when the Bible says to let the wheat and the tares grow, I believe that He wants us to live peaceably with all men and trust that God will bring the separation when the time is right because if we were to separate from them ourselves, God knows, we would make a mess out of everything. We must love everyone and sometimes the people that fight you the most are the ones closest to you and the ones you should be helping the most.

When your heart is not right you are not right. I had to learn this the hard way, I used to hold people in my heart that had hurt me and I realized that by holding on to all these hurts and pain I was setting myself up for a heart failure spiritually and naturally. See in the natural the heart is a small organ and it was not created to bear heavy burdens, so it is in the spirit realm and I believe that is why the Lord told us not to worry about anything because he knows how much we can bear.

My heart condition started to get better as the days go by because I started to let go of things, I no longer walk in defeat, because I am more than a conqueror, I no longer engage in backbiting and gossip, and I can see how much the Lord has brought me through.

I am not afraid to say my heart was corrupt; I was on my way to hell because of all the unforgiveness I was holding, I was walking in defeat, but I thank the Lord that He did not take me out in my mess and believe it or not He will do the same for you. Make up your mind today to release from your heart, all those who hurt you, disappointed or where not there when you needed them. Once you do this you are well on your way to having a pure heart.

But God

A new commandment I give unto you, That ye love one another; as I have loved you, that ye also love one another. By this shall all men know that ye are my disciples, if ye have love one to another. John 13:34-45

was reading Facebook one day and saw my daughter Danisha put on her status that "The keys to success is not having titles, or drive, or ambition but is putting Jesus First and doing the will of the Father" I get so tickled with all these titles, it's all good to be an Apostle, Evangelist or even Deacon but don't you know that our titles don't impress God? Neither does it destroy the devil!

We can't fool ourselves for a moment although we all sometime or another may have thought of ourself on a higher level than others because of a title, but I once heard someone say that you have the Bachelors degree and holding the title of a leader in the Church but have no power, no love, no compassion, full of envy and jealousy, you are just wasting your time. You should be living a life that is pleasing to God so that others will want to and will follow.

I am not trying to condemn anyone but I rather have JESUS than degrees. Please do not think I am saying that having a degree is not important, I would be lying because I am still in college working on my first degree, but what I mean is that no matter what position you hold in life or in the Church you should treat everyone with love.

Sometimes God watches to see how we treat each other, I have had some really bad experiences with leaders but one thing that I never did was let it drive me up the wall or cause me to walk away from God. I say this because the Church is a hospital for the lost and they should be able to enter in and feel loved but unfortunately we sometimes forget where God brought us from and where we could have been.

I thank the Lord for all that He brought me through, I praise Him because of who He is, so if you are out there and you are not saved and you say, well I am going to serve the Lord after I finish school and accomplish my goals or maybe you are saved and a leader in the Church and you might say, *"Lord*

I will treat others better after my promotion." You are on the wrong track, you have to get it right NOW because tomorrow is not promised. Give your life TODAY, love your brother and sisters TODAY, forgive and forget TODAY, and a real touchy one that we fail to admit is that we should BE HAPPY for others, get rid of envy and jealousy TODAY. Jesus loves us all and He is not a respecter of persons, but the question is, DO YOU LOVE HIM?

We are so caught up with ourselves that we forget about what the word of God says, in 1 Peter 4:80 *"Above all, love each other deeply, because love covers over a multitude of sins."* I remember when there was a time in my life when I felt like giving up, when I felt like all hope was gone and I remember when there was no one to turn to, BUT GOD!

When you have been scarred by your own brother and sisters, it makes you put up a wall and we know that is not God, No way! Because no matter the hurt we MUST let it go. We have to forgive and move along. People you trusted the most hurt you and you now have to be in the same building worshipping and praising God with them, but I believe that it is the will of the Father that we lay aside every malice, every hate, let go of all tension and allow the Holy Spirit to saturate our hearts and permeate our minds so the love of God can be seen in us and through us. It's only by His Grace why we are alive so value every moment of life and place the lies of the enemy under your feet.

When I think of all the pain and the hurts that I have been through, my friends, I have to say thank you Lord, He has never let me down. He does not always come when you want Him BUT He is always on time.

During my days of struggle He spoke into my Spirit and let me know that He is with me and He will never leave me nor forsake me, He showed me that as long as I put Him first He will be my guide, so I am here to remind some and to inform others that your titles don't define who you are, you are bought with a price.

So let's get it together because there are so many hurting souls out there and yet we are so busy fighting and competing against each other.

We are the light of the world so we need to allow the Holy Spirit to shine through us and forget about our titles, forget about ourselves and let God use us to save that person that is on the verge of suicide, that mother that is homeless, that father that lost his job, let us come together and show the world that we are children of the most high God and we will not settle for less. Many of us were in similar situations or could have been BUT GOD...

In Due Season

For the vision is yet for an appointed time, but at the end it shall speak, and not lie: though it tarry, wait for it; because it will surely come, it will not tarry. Habakkuk 2:3

Sometimes we disregard what people say to us because we are familiar with the person, but I hear the word of God say that *a Prophet is without honor, save in his own country,* and I can truly say that I was guilty for a while.

About five years ago, a dear friend of mine prophesied to me and told me before witnesses that the Lord showed her that I will be getting married and my husband will be a pastor, I heard the word but in all truth I did not receive the word because I did not see the prophetic in her, but my friends you don't need a celebrity prophet to come in and speak a word over your life, the Lord can use whomever He chooses. Truthfully all you need is to be in tune with the Spirit and allow the Lord to use His humble servants in the area of their gifting. I tell you that it was while I was on the set of my TV Show that someone who was there reminded me of the word.

When God speaks His Word cannot return void it will come to pass. The point is that she was correct because I did get married and my husband is now being sent out to pastor his own flock, so what I am trying to say is that we shouldn't judge a book by it's cover and another thing I learned is that even though she knew I did not pay attention to what she said she never gave up, she delivered the word and did not get easily offended.

Do not allow people to determine what you do for God. Your job is to obey God regardless of what people say. The same thing was true of Jesus. The crowds loved Jesus, but the Pharisees did not.

I am now married to my husband and it has been an adventure and I know that God has placed us into each other's path for a purpose. Nothing good comes without a fight, it was a fight to get him and it's a spiritual fight to keep him.

As women we sometimes live in a little fantasy but my adventure began on January 5, 2008 when I said "I DO."

My hubby, a Minister of the Gospel, a Captain in the United States Army, an Author and the list goes on, has been my greatest support. I can truly say that he came into my life at a time when God saw the need. A lot of people saw me coming to Church faithfully every Sunday and Tuesday and little did they know that I was going through a really hard time of my life, it bring tears to my eyes when I think about the pain I was going through, but I learned one thing about myself and that was that I am more than a conqueror. I learned that God will not place on you more than you can bear and as long as you have the Lord on your side, everything else is history.

Larry came into my life and everything changed. I felt a love that I never felt before. I dare to sit here and paint a picture perfect but despite our differences he is truly a man after God's own heart. He has pulled out the things that the Lord has placed in me and he has been so encouraging in all my endeavors. I know that my destiny is attached to Larry Birchett, Jr.

The way we met was a set-up from God and I

am so grateful for my blessing. God is not a respecter of persons and I believe that God wants to blow your mind too, but you can't be hung up over who walked out. Don't you know that light attracts light and only people that like the light will be able to stay connected to you?

After being married for four years, one thing that I have learned is that you have to treat the man of God with love and respect. As women we get emotional sometimes and the men on the other hand they have big egos but if we stay in our lanes and position ourselves in order, we will see result. God knows I am still a work in progress, but I am willing to allow God to reconstruct me, and during this process I will keep on doing His will.

Discipleship

And Jesus saith unto them, Follow me, and I will make you fishers of men. Matthew 4:19

The Lord has dropped in my Spirit to speak on this subject because so many times we give up on people. We don't take the time to minister to the lost. I sometimes cannot understand how we keep God to ourselves in a box, when the Lord has called us to make disciples of ALL men. Are you doing the will of the Father? Well, let's find out.

What is Discipleship? This is the intensely personal activity of two or more persons helping each other experience a growing relationship with God.

A Disciple is a follower, one that accepts and assists.

Discipleship is more than being a believer or having a title it's about being a follower of Christ! Once we make a decision for Christ, then just like Matthew,

Peter and Mary Magdalene we must follow Him and make others His disciples too. The Bible says Greater Works we shall do and when we study the Word of God we see all the different miracles that Jesus did and yet He tells us that we shall do Greater things.

I pondered on this for a moment and realized that in order to do these works we must become rooted and grounded in Him. We have to study the word and hide it in our hearts.

1 Thess. 5:11 states that we should encourage others, build up one another, commend each other and not condemn.

Jesus' primary call to His Disciples is seen in His words

1. **COME TO ME** ------ MATT 11:28
2. **FOLLOW ME** ------- MATT 4:19

Jesus' relationship with His Disciples precedes His assignment to them because He loved them. And we need Love one for another according to John 13: 34 "A new commandment I give unto you, that ye love one another; as I have loved you, that ye also love one another"

In Matt 28:19-20 He gave them the great Commission which was to GO, TEACH AND BAPTIZE. Making disciples involves these 3 steps. How can we do this if we are not on one accord or we don't show the love of God to each other? We have to be on one accord my brothers and sisters in order for the Holy Spirit to work through us. We must be useable and available.

Beloved I am only here to encourage you while I encourage myself and if we work together we can win nations for the Kingdom because remember that he that winneth souls is wise, and being children of the Most High God we are destined for success.

Here are a few nuggets I would like to leave you with:

A disciple must have assurance of salvation. He must know that he is a child of God that Christ dwells within him.

A disciple walks in the fullness and power of the Holy Spirit. The Holy Spirit is responsible for everything that happens in the life of a believer-his new birth, daily walk, understanding of Scripture, and prayers. He produces the fruit of the Spirit in us, which enables us to live holy lives and witness for Christ.

A disciple demonstrates love for God, his neighbor, his fellow disciples, and his enemies. Jesus commands us to love God with all of our hearts, with all of our souls, with all of our minds, and he also commands us to love our neighbors as ourselves.

A disciple is one who knows how to read, study, memorize, and meditate upon the Word of God, to hide its truths in his heart. It is impossible to walk in the fullness of God's Holy Spirit without an understanding of God's Word. The reverse is also true-you can't understand God's Word without the Holy Spirit.

A true disciple of Jesus is a man or woman of prayer. The Lord Jesus Christ, who spent 40 days in prayer and fasting in the wilderness, is our great example of this.

The disciple is one who is obedient, who studies the Word of God, and obeys the commands of God in a lifestyle that honors the Lord Jesus Christ.

A disciple is one who trusts God and lives a life of faith. Scripture reminds us that "without faith it is impossible to please God."

A disciple understands God's grace. God loves us unconditionally, whether we obey him or not. This is the opposite of legalism, the primary heresy of the Christian life, which urges us to try to obey God's laws in our own wisdom, our own strength, and our own power.

A disciple is one who witnesses for Christ as a way of life. As Christians we are to bear fruit, according to John 15:8. This includes the fruit of souls brought into Christ's kingdom as well as the fruit of the Spirit.

A true disciple of the Lord Jesus worships God in the fellowship of his church. He is involved in his church through study, worship, prayer, tithing, witnessing, and the stewardship of his time, talent, and treasure.

If you want to become a disciple of our Savior and be a disciple of others, you can begin today. Develop the practice of spending time alone each day with God in prayer and in his Word. Ask the Lord to remove the thorns in your flesh so your mindset can change, pray for people who will meet on a day to day basis, and commit yourself to changing the world through evangelism and discipleship. The world desperately needs such a change, but only our Lord Jesus Christ has the power and plan to change people and nations.

Moments of Silence

Fear ye not, stand still, and see the salvation of the LORD,
which he will shew to you to day: for the Egyptians whom
ye have seen to day, ye shall see them again no more for
ever.Exodus 14:13

*H*ave you ever woke up and felt like *"Lord, where* *are you? And what do I do now?"* Well I have had some of those days when I have felt as though I was not in the right place. There are times in my life when I get the feeling, *Am I supposed to be here? Am I in your will Lord? Where do I go from here?* But I have learned that it's those moments that I have to push past my feelings and emotions and allow the Lord to minister to me like only He knows how.

When God places you in a family, whether Church family or even your own natural family it's for a reason and the thing about families is that you don't get to choose your family. I woke up one morning July 12, 1970 into the Ottey family, then the Lord placed me in the True United family but He did not stop there, On January 5, 2008, He placed me into the Birchett family and while He was still transitioning me He placed me into the Brand New Life Family.

Sometimes you never know what God is doing, you will never understand the move of God but in those times I have learned to be silent and be still. I realize that there are some things that you cannot share with everyone, because not everyone has your best interest at heart. Someone who has never been where you have been most times cannot relate.

If you were never on the verge of getting evicted with your kids, you will never understand what it feels like but I do! There was a time when I had no one to turn to and I had to put ALL my trust in GOD. I had to trust Him when the electric got cut off, when I lost my job as a single mom, when there was no other source of income.

Sometimes I look back at the hardship that I went through and it makes me realize that in those times I did not run to anyone but I kept silent. I laughed when there were no jokes. I had to let my children know that God is able. I know that life has its ups and downs; it has struggles, but God was my guide, even when I could not understand where He was leading me.

The Lord will test your endurance to see where your faith lies. You cannot allow anyone or anything to cause you to delay what He has for you, after you have done all you can, STAND!

That is the word, so on that note, devil, let's get ready to rumble!

Through the Storms

Whosoever cometh to me, and heareth my sayings, and doeth them, I will shew you to whom he is like: He is like a man which built an house, and digged deep, and laid the foundation on a rock: and when the flood arose, the stream beat vehemently upon that house, and could not shake it: for it was founded upon a rock. Luke 6:47-48

When you find yourself in a storm it's no time to have pity parties or get weak, a storm comes not to break you but to make you stronger.

Storms come in all different ways they are also considered as light afflictions and the word of God says: *"For our light affliction, which is but for a moment, worketh for us a far more exceeding and eternal weight of glory' 2 Corinthians 4:17*

And many are the afflictions of the righteous; But God will deliver them from all, Psalm 34:6

These trials and tribulations are just test of our faith.

Our storms cause us to trust in God and surrender to the Lord God, the pain, the trials, the tears the issues all hurt and yes they get heavy but we must still trust in God. Why? He will never give us more than we can bear and that is biblical.

When I think about how the Lord kept me through so many storms in my life, Wow! That's all I can say because a lot of you might not know but I was stuck up twice at gun point and it was GOD that kept me alive! One time a trash bag was placed over my head, I could not breathe, I had to bite a hole in the bag in order to survive, that is why I praise God the way I do, because I owe my life to him.

So if you are reading this today and you are going through any storms in your life, take a step back and consider JESUS, let him be your protector, let him cover you. If I was not saved then and he kept me, how much more now will he hide me no matter what storm comes my way.

Many times we ask God to deliver us out of the storms but I believe that God allows things to happen for a reason, when I look at the struggles of Job whose back was up against the wall, he lost everything but not his soul because he trusted in God, to trust God means to surrender your all to him, simply means that you don't rely on yourself or anyone but all your faith is in him.

Proverbs 3:5 states *"Trust in the Lord with all your heart and lean not on your own understanding."*

Do you know that if we follow the word of God we will overcome, we will fulfill the scripture that says 'we are more than a conquerer' a quitter cannot win and a winner cannot quit so therefore let us stand on the word of God and believe by faith that *"All things work together for the good of them that love him and that are called according to his purpose."* Romans 8:28

Another way to completely trust in God is by knowing him, we have to have a intimate relationship with the father, otherwise we are fooling ourselves, you cannot trust what you don't believe or obey,

The bible say *"be ye holy because I am holy"* 1 Peter 1: 16

This is no joke my friends we have to trust and obey because there is no other way.

Hebrews 13:6 So we can say with confidence, "The Lord is my helper; I will not be afraid. What can anyone do to me?" Can you imagine how things could improve in our lives if we put God first and trusted him?

I remember one Saturday afternoon, on our way to Delaware the brakes went on our car, the caliper broke and we were in a high volume of traffic, if it was not for the grace and mercy of God, we would have been dead, so I don't really care how people see me it's what God says about me that makes the difference.

His Presence

And the LORD said, My presence shall go with thee, and I will give thee rest. ~ Exodus 33:14

When I think about His presence it makes my heart skip a beat, just to know that He loves me and He wants the best for me is assurance that I am blessed.

I was at home one day and the thought came to me about one night in His presence, all it takes is one night and your whole life will be changed, you will not be the same again, I always wondered how people can be in Praise and Worship and they are busy doing other things, the Lord showed me that we do not bring His presence in He is already there and when we praise Him it invokes His presence and prepares us to get into a worship realm where we get ready to go into the Holy of Holies.

I believe that when we worship on one accord and the Lord sees love and unity His presence will be able to flow and manifest freely and people will be filled, lives will be changed and we will never be the same again.

About 12 years ago I went to Church because I was religious; I would only go at certain times, Christmas, New Year and Easter, but one night I felt a different feeling and I had to walk down to the altar. That feeling was the presence of God. I was never the same again. My mindset was changed, my attitude starting changing and all I wanted was more of Him; more of the love and security that I had felt.

I don't know what you are facing today, but I know a man that is able to keep you from all your enemies. He will resurrect every dry area in your life; He raises the dead, He heals the sick, He washes away our sins. He is the God of today, tomorrow and forever more. He is God all by Himself and His love last forever. Once you accept Him as your personal Savior He will enter your heart and be your guide. Jesus Christ loves you and me so much that He hung and died on a cross, if that wasn't enough He rose again and gave us a second chance to get it right. What a mighty God!

If I don't tell you about this Man I would not be doing what He has called me to do, so I ask you today are you saved? Have you accepted Jesus as your Lord and Savior? If your answer is no then there is still hope, accept Him today. Once you accept Him as your Lord and Savior, He will enter into your heart and you will began to experience His awesome Presence.

Please say this prayer after me:

Dear Lord, I am sorry, I have sinned against you and you only, please forgive me of all my flaws, cleanse me of all unrighteous, I renounce satan from my life and I accept you as my Lord and Savior from this day on and forever more, in Jesus Name. Amen

If you have said this prayer and meant it from your heart, then you are saved, so now you need to find a bible believing Church and get baptized and I pray that the Lord will bless you and keep you in his presence.

You are a Winner!

But thanks be to God, which giveth us the victory through our Lord Jesus Christ.~1 Corinthians 15:57

I got up one morning to do my daily morning run and as I took each stride I felt the presence of the Lord. I opened my mouth and said "Speak Lord!" Immediately He began to tell me the reason He allowed some of the things to happen in my life was so that He might get the GLORY from my life. Sudden painful and confusing times began to make sense.

The Lord has done so much for us and no matter what we go through we have to always remember He is Lord and He will never allow the enemy to triumph over us!!! He watches over us. *I cannot imagine life without Him.*

When life struggles come, the Lord is always here to provide a way of escape, you have to realize that all things happen for a reason and through it all if you can just hold on **you will win**!

There was a time in my life since I have been married, that I felt like all the doors were closing in on us, but I am so blessed for the husband that the Lord gave me because he has always maintained a positive outlook on things, despite us having to lose two cars having to do a short sale on our home and various other trials we have gone through God has been faithful and has shown Himself to be a restorer. So despite what the bill collector might say, we trust in the Lord.

It is one thing to know you should have faith but faith untested is not really faith. Our faith was tried on *every side* and because of our faithfulness in God, He opened up the flood gates and released His blessings on us. I am not saying that we have it all together but with God all things are possible. Just know He is working everything out for your good and His Glory and **yes I am talking to you**!

I know that I am called to nations and sometimes it's a fight to do the will of God but I have made up in my mind that whatever He says I will do. See when I was not serving him I was running in the world doing things that edified my flesh. I made so much money that I should be a millionaire right now but the Lord showed me that all that I did then He wants me to do now but in a different manner and I will be doing it for His GLORY!

All the money I made then will not be able to be compared to the souls I will be winning for His Kingdom. That hunger and drive that I had for the things of this world has been replaced and consumed by the things of God.

Your method might not be the same as mine but we can all do this together. God loves us all and we are all winners, we are children of the most high God and no matter what trial or tribulation comes your way, just know that you can encourage yourself to keep going and keep pushing. It's the enemy job to steal kill and destroy and if there is no opposition, you need to check your spirit.

Through the grace, mercy and love of God, I overcame all my haters, all my hurts, all my pains, and everything the enemy ever told me that was a lie. I now try to live a life where God gets the Glory from it, the road is not easy my friends **but it is worth it**. If Jesus bore the cross, we can too.

He has equipped us to be winners; you are not a quitter, because quitters never win and winners never quit, we already have the victory and guess what? You cannot allow people or situation to delay you from stepping into what God has in store for you, don't you know that we are gems in disguise?

My brothers and sisters I thank you for reading this vision that the Lord gave me and I encourage you today that no matter what, He knows the plans He has for you. His word cannot return to Him void. Be content in whatever situation you are in because happiness is external but joy comes from deep within.

To all my single sisters and brothers, we sometimes get easily defeated because we fail to plan but one thing I learned is that in order to be victorious you must have the Word of God in your hearts and then you will have Good Success. So as you wait on the 'one' the Lord has for you start planning how you are going to be as a husband or a wife and how you want your spouse to be. Just make sure you use the Word of God as your manual! Always remember that a man or woman is not your source of joy, God is and until you find joy in Him, you won't find joy in anyone else.

To my married sisters and brothers, love and cherish each other, treat each other with great respect whatever you give you will receive, the word of God tells us whatever we sow that shall we also reap.

You are a survivor, winning is your destiny, so get yourself up shake yourself loose and reclaim your identity by being the man or woman of God that God created you to be. Claim your position, walk as a woman or man of greatness, you are an original design, and there is nothing or no one that can make you lose because **Defeat is NEVER an option**!

Defeat Is Not an Option

Living as a child of God has its ups and downs
But nobody said it would be easy
The race was not given to the weak but to the strong
Just hold on, have faith because the victory is already won
God has changed our walk and our identity
Our past should not uproot our future
It's easier to face your past when you are fighting for your future
Your past did not disqualify you but it solidified you
Be ready because
Perception becomes reality and Christ is our firm foundation
Therefore defeat is not an option
So look the devil in his face and let him know the fight is on and
we are Armed and Dangerous
We are soldiers in the army of the Lord.

In this fight there will be thorns that dig into your flesh
But God won't give you more than you can bear
Because His Grace is sufficient for you
Your finances may be shaky,
But He will supply all you need according to His riches in Glory.
Sickness might take over your body
But by His stripes we are healed
So you see, we are destined to win
There is no place for defeat
Remember this one thing and know that God's mercies preceded
His judgment
He is an omnipotent, omnipresent God
And with Him all things are possible
So I stand here to say
Devil bring it on
Defeat is not an option
No way, No how

Written by Joanna Birchett ~ February 2010

SEVEN DAYS
of
MEDITATIONS

Seven Days Of Meditations

I pray that this book was able to open your minds to realize that when you have the Lord on your side it doesn't matter who is against you. You will *never* lose; you have to believe that you are *more* than a conqueror.

Remember my beloved, no matter what season you might be in right now, it won't last always, don't give in, don't quit, don't throw in the towel, you can make it, and I prayerfully leave with you these seven devotionals for you to meditate on daily, I chose to do seven days because 7 is the number for completion and they helped me in the different seasons that I went through, so please allow the Lord to minister to you through these meditations and reflections.

Day 1

Love

Of all the things that God is; He is *Love* and as children of the most high God we are to show love one to another. So what if they stepped on your toes today or talked about you behind your back. I know all this hurts the natural man but we walk not in the flesh so therefore we are supposed to stop for a moment and ask ourselves the question, what would Jesus do in this situation? Is the love of God showing through me?

The bible says that we should be imitators of Christ so therefore Love is a principal thing in being a follower of Christ. Love is patient and kind.

Apply this in your life on a daily basis and perception will become reality. Ask the Lord to teach you to love just like He loves you and remember that this kind of love is God's Character.

*If I speak in the tongues of men or of angels, but do not
have love, I am only a resounding
gong or a clanging cymbal.~ 1Corinthians 13:1*

Meditate and Reflect:
~Love~

Is the love of God visible in your life?

Take time out of your schedule and show someone that you love them just because.

Love is a doing word and you can feel when someone is really showing you love, we tend to use this word loosely and I think it's because some people don't know what true love really is, True love shows compassion, it is not envious, it does not boast , it is faithful and we can go on, this real love comes from the Lord which is the Agape Love, a love that's unconditional and the Bible tells us that we should show love one to another, it doesn't matter how he/she has hurt you or how they treated you, allow the love of God that's within you to be shown one to another and be real about it.

A new commandment I give to you, that you love one another: just as I have loved you, you also are to love one another. By this all people will know that you are my disciples, if you have love for one another." ~ John 13:34-35

Day 2

Forgiveness

A heart that forgives is what the psalmist sings but let's get real, is it that easy? Forgiveness is a huge subject and certainly one in which the Bible is not silent. In the Bible we can read about our amazing and loving Heavenly Father who forgives us of all trespasses.

Unforgiveness is a common sin and it breeds other bad habits so learning to let go of things quickly, makes a great difference and this allows the Holy Spirit to take control of whatever the situation might be. I believe that God's heart gets grieved at the way we treat each other, how can you say you love the Lord when you cannot even forgive?

You cannot allow anyone to cause you to delay what God has in store for you by holding unforgiveness in your heart. Let go and let God take control of your mind, your body and your soul, Know this brethren that God's character is forgiving. Our attitude should be loving and forgiving just like God forgave you.

Be kind to one another, tenderhearted, forgiving one another, as God in Christ forgave you. ~Ephesians 4:32

Meditate and Reflect:

~Forgiveness~

What if I don't forgive?

Why should I forgive him/her when they did me wrong? He /she walked out on me, he/she talked badly about me.

I understand how you might feel but when we don't forgive we "give the devil a chance to work on" us and we are handed over to the torturers (Mt 18:34).

These torturers are such things as fear, loneliness, depression, frustration, anxiety, and self-hatred, so we have to follow the Word and do what Jesus did, on the cross He said "Father forgive them."

No matter how people hurt us, or abuse us we have to have a heart that forgives and forgets because if we persist in unforgiveness, we cut ourselves off from God forever and thereby damn ourselves.

My brothers and sisters Release it today!

Day 3

Never Give Up

All my life I was taught not to give up, never throw in the towel and as an adult I always have that in mind. I remember one night I was home with the kids and the enemy was playing tricks on my mind, but the Lord used a friend to call at a moment when I needed a little encouragement, and it was after the phone call that I recognized that God is amazing.

I began to worship from the depth of my very soul and at that very moment I felt a peace come over me and I know you can relate to this, because we all have been there a time or two. Sometimes it can be hard to encourage yourself but it is always possible.

I say this to let someone know today that all is not lost, just press and have expectancy in your heart when you go before the Lord. Remember expectancy breeds miracles? YES! You want God to move in your life but do you really believe that He can and is able to do it? If you really believe it then Never Give Up!

Let us not become weary in doing good, for at the proper time we will reap a harvest if we do not give up. Galatians 6:9 (NIV)

Meditate and Reflect:

~Never Give up~

I don't know what to do, everything is so wrong in my life, I cannot go on anymore.

You don't understand how I feel, you are not going through it, I am and I don't see any change coming.

Things don't seem to be working out for you, you are at a cross road in your life and you feel like giving up, but come to tell you today my sister, my brother that all is not gone, you are destined for greatness, you are more than a conqueror, you cannot give up now.

Your storms are not allowed to kill you; they are allowed to make you stronger, you notice that I said ALLOWED, that's because God knows all things He holds your life in the palm of His hands so you best believe that He will not allow you to give up or throw in the towel, He did not create no quitters!

Day 4

A Season of Solitude

Sometimes we find ourselves feeling lonely and all left out but it is then that God can speak to us and download everything that He needs for us to do.

The bible state in Psalm 94:22 that the Lord is our Defense and our Refuge. He promised that He would not leave us nor forsake us He is our strong tower and when the days seems long and dreary He is our comfort and shield so we have no reason to worry or get discouraged, when we find ourselves in a season of Solitude just know that God is still in control. Remember that God is your daily bread and the restorer of your Joy. He is the Great I Am and His word cannot return to Him void! Why? Because He is GOD!

So I can assure you that whatever state you are in RIGHT NOW speak life and wait for the results. You are the Prophet of your own life, (Quote from Kenneth Copeland) and you shall have just what you say.

God has said "Never will I leave you; never will I forsake you"
Hebrews 13:56 (NIV)

Meditate and Reflect:

~A Season of Solitude~

Are you at this place in your life? And you are saying these things:

Sometimes I get the feeling like I am in a place all alone, and nobody cares or even understands. Lord, where are you?

Sometimes we all have these days but I can assure you that when you get this feeling it's time to get on your knees, get into your secret place and just be still. Solitude doesn't always mean a bad thing, it might be a time when God is trying to get your attention because your schedule is so crowded. Allow the Lord to speak to you and just sit and listen to Him minister to you.

Day 5

The Lord My Shepherd

Wow! When I think of the sheep and how the shepherd watches over them night and day, it excites me because we have our own shepherd, the Lord God Almighty, the great I AM, He watches over us twenty four seven, He never slumbers nor sleep.

I am so grateful for His presence always watching over me, even when He is silent I rest assured that the shepherd is watching over me. I remember one Saturday my family and I were on our way to Delaware and lo and behold the brakes went on the car, the car would not stop and my husband who was driving kept honking the horn because he had to go through the lights, he swerved and did all he could, but it was the Lord that was on our side, the Lord our Shepherd, our way maker that protected us.

I am so glad that He knows us by name and nature. He will watch over you and yours if you let Him.

The Lord is my shepherd I shall not want ~Psalm 23:1

Meditate and Reflect:

~The Lord Is My Shepherd~

Is the Lord watching over me? Am I one of his sheep?

I cannot hear from the Lord and I have to do something about this situation now!

I hear the Lord saying that that He is your Shepherd and He will never leave you neither will he forsake you. He is a good Shepherd who knows how to watch over His sheep.

The Bible says that "My Sheep hears my voice and a stranger he will not follow" John 10:27. When we allow God our Shepherd to guide us it brings us a peace, contentment because we know that we are safe. But when we choose to sin, we go our own wayward way and we cannot blame the Shepherd because He gives us choices.

Our Shepherd knows the "green pastures" and "quiet waters" that will build us up and restore us. Rebelling against the shepherd will only lead destruction, please to go remember this the next time that you get tempted your own way instead of the Lord's way. If you are reading this and you have a desire to know this Shepherd that I am talking about, just close your eyes and welcome him in and he will enter into your heart today and find a Church where the name of the Lord is high and lifted up!

Day 6

Pursuit of My Purpose

Every one has a purpose, the bible says that "The Earth is the Lord's and the fullness thereof the world and they that dwell therein" so all things was created by God and all things are created for a purpose. Individually we are created for different things but corporately, we are all created for one purpose here on earth and that's to give the Lord Glory.

So when the days get rough and dreary, just remember that you have a purpose, despite what the enemy cries, God has a plan and a purpose for your life and it will work together for your good and God's Glory.

Always be in pursuit of your purpose because you are fearfully and wonderfully made in God's image and I can tell you right now that you can read all the books you can, they will encourage and edify you but you cannot find your purpose in a book.

Many are the plans in a person's heart, but it is the Lord's purpose that prevails. ~ Proverbs 19:21

Meditate and Reflect:

~Pursuit of My Purpose~

Why was I created?

I don't believe that there is purpose in my life.

We all have asked these things at a point in ou. life and man cannot answer these questions for us, w have to develop and build a personal relationship with the Father, and He will mold us into who He ha: created us to be, your purpose is different than mine: but I believe that we were all created to give Glory unt the Lord.

I am not here to tell you that I have arrived int my purpose but I am in pursuit of whatever the Lor has in store for me, these questions that you have ar pushing you to your purpose. They're pointing you ir the direction of a specific purpose. Now don't get m wrong we don't have all the answers but if we get ir line with the Word of God He will reveal all things to u in time.

Day 7

You have God's Favor

*G*od's favor lasts for a lifetime and despite what others say, His favor will carry you today, tomorrow and forever more.

There are so many times in my life that I can remember the favor of God allowing doors to open and you best believe that when God open the door no man can close them, His favor is beyond compare. We don't deserve it but he loves us so much that he looks beyond ALL our faults and bless us anyhow, WHAT A GOD! Sometimes we don't realize how much favor God grants us daily:

He woke you up this morning ~ *THAT'S FAVOR*

He clothed you in your right minds ~ *THAT'S FAVOR*

After all is said and done, all the pain and trials you bear, but you don't look like the things that you been through, you need to lift your voice and say *I HAVE GOD'S FAVOR!*

His anger is but for a moment; But His Favor lasts for a lifetime ~ Psalm 30:5 (NIV)

Meditate and Reflect

~ God's Favor~

So if I am favored by God, how come I am struggling so much?

Why did he/ walk out and left me with the kids?

What is Favor?

God's Favor is for a lifetime and one thing that would like to say is that favor does not stop trials or tribulations, the Bible says that *they that are Godly must suffer persecution* so I see here that even though the storms are raging and we are pressed on every side.

God still has favor on your life, He woke you up to another day, He provides food and shelter, He opens doors no man can close, you best believe that's the favor of God, you are **blessed**!

No matter how you look at the situation, when you are a child of God you have a covenant with the Father and therefore favor follows you wherever you go.

My Prayer

I pray that these meditations will impact your life and cause a shift in your spirit. I encourage you to use them as the Lord leads you and according to your needs. They were written from my heart and I believe that the Lord will be glorified through these seven meditations. One thing I know is that we all struggle in an area or two and it's nothing to be ashamed of because God loves you even with your flaws, but if you desire a change, a move, a shift in your life, you have to be consistent with the things that the Lord places in your heart. God is verbal and He speaks, so get in the habit of praying and then meditate on His words and during your meditation make sure you are listening for the voice of the Lord.

Father, I come before your people and I first ask you to forgive me of all my flaws, all my emotional feelings, allow your Holy Spirit to saturate me RIGHT NOW LORD! Build a hedge of protection around our hearts and minds, so that we will not sin against you, I thank you in advance for the blessings of the Lord that maketh rich and adds no sorrow. Father I love you, I honor you, I adore you, you are worthy to be praised!! Hallelujah Jesus, so because of who you are Lord I lift your name on high, Lord I ask you to bless someone today as they read this book, open up their understanding and I pray this book be used to restore brokenness, heal the sick and transform lives, all these mercies I pray IN JESUS NAME AMEN!

To correspond with Evangelist Joanna Birchett

You are free to contact her through email

gospel4uministry@gmail.com

Or visit her on the web at
www.gospel4uministry@gmail.com

Made in the USA
Charleston, SC
19 May 2013